Rus

The Inspirational Story of Football Superstar Russell Wilson

Table Of Contents

Introduction

As the title already implies, this is a short book about [The Inspirational Story of Football Superstar Russell Wilson] and how he rose from his life in the Richmond, Virginia area to becoming one of today's leading and most-respected football players. In his rise to superstardom, Russell has inspired not only the youth, but fans of all ages throughout the world.

This book also portrays the struggles that Russell has had to overcome during his early childhood and teen years, all the way up until he became who he is today. A notable source of inspiration is Russell's own foundation that was named after him, as well as his consistent support of other charitable organizations, such as the Children's Hospital. He continues to serve as the humble superstar in a sport that glorifies flashy plays and mega personalities.

Combining incredible accuracy, sharp decision-making, quick feet, and superior coordination, Russell has shown the ability to slice up just about any form of defense. From being a young two-sport athlete, to becoming one of the greatest young quarterbacks of his generation, you'll learn here how this man has risen to the ranks of the best football players today.

Thanks again for grabbing this book. Hopefully you are able to take some lessons from Russell's story and apply them to your own life!

Chapter 1:

Early Childhood and Youth

Russell Wilson was born on November 29th, 1988 in Cincinnati, Ohio. He comes from a multiracial background with predominantly African American ancestry. His father, Harrison Benjamin Wilson III, was a lawyer, while his mother, Tammy, was a legal nurse consultant.

Russell grew up with two siblings: An older brother, Harrison IV, and a younger sister, Anna. The Wilson family was heavily athletic; Russell began to play football with his father and older brother at the age of four.

Russell's grandfather, who was once the president at Norfolk State University, played football and baseball for Kentucky State University. His father also played football at Dartmouth, while his older brother played for the University of Richmond. Even Russell's sister, Anna, was one of the most highly-rated basketball prospects in America.

Now that we know Russell was born into a family of athletes, it seems pretty obvious why he started to take an interest in sports at a very young age. He even started calling plays in fourth grade; he had no problem leading other children. Wilson's teachers would often say that he was very assertive in school.

Russell grew up in a very close-knit family. He spent almost all of his free time playing sports with his older brother. Tammy, his mother, would recall both of her sons playing outside for the entire day many times. Russell found it difficult to beat his older brother, Harry, and would often complain about losing, but would never give up on any game. Tammy said Harry really helped Russell become stronger and develop character because Harry never let Russell win. This helped to bring out the best in Russell, and forced him to learn about hard work and overcoming obstacles.

While Russell always excelled in sports, his parents also made sure that he took his studies seriously. His mother would help him with his Math and Science subjects, while his father supported him in English and History.

Russell knew how to use his skills in sports to help him with his studies. By the seventh grade, he began to leverage his friends in order to improve his academics: He would help his friends in whatever athletic skill they were trying to develop, and in return, they helped him develop better studying habits.

The traits that Russell exhibited at a young age prove to be what he still excels at as a professional. Many people around the NFL praise Russell's work ethic and leadership abilities. We now know that these traits began to develop in his early childhood years, and his family played a vital role in both his physical and personal development.

Russell's father also instilled in him a sense that someone was always watching over him – and also watching what he was saying. As a young boy of seven, Russell's father would coach him during simulated press conferences, running through questions and answers. This led Russell to be careful about not saying the wrong thing, and to be always on the message when he opens his mouth.

Chapter 2:

High School and College Career

For high school, Russell attended the Collegiate School in Richmond, Virginia. He was in the 10th grade when something memorable happened. Wilson and a 6' 5" 11th grader were both trying out for the quarterback position on the football team. The coach decided to let them compete for the spot, and devised a game to decide on who would be the starting quarterback.

Russell won the game that his coach devised and became the starting quarterback for the team. This was the first time that Russell really felt that he could overcome his height and become a great quarterback by developing other intangibles. It was a huge step for Russell's confidence, and it gave him the feeling that his height was not a limitation for the ceiling of his football career.

Russell proved that he deserved the spot in the following years of his high school career. As a junior, he managed to score 40 total touchdowns and developed some thickness to his frame. He began to read defenses better and it was shown in the team's overall production. He was named an All-District and All-State player. Russell was even given the Richmond Times Dispatch Player of the Year award. After his junior year, the team was clearly his, and he took his leadership to the next level. He knew that he would have a huge impact on how the team's season would turn out, and so he developed his game even further.

As a senior, Russell threw for 34 touchdowns with seven interceptions. He was also featured in Sports Illustrated for his incredible performances. Additionally, he was chosen as the Class President during his senior year of high school. The fact that he was able to become an amazing football and baseball star *and* become the class president told a lot about his work ethic and personality at such a young age.

After his senior year of high school, Russell was given a scholarship offer to play football for the North Carolina State Wolfpack football team as a student-athlete. It was a dream come true for Russell, and he took the offer.

Wilson redshirted his freshman year of college. "Redshirting" is a term used in U.S. collegiate sports where an athlete's eligibility is extended for up to two years. Red shirt students can attend classes at a university and practice for an athletic team, but are not allowed to compete in games. The main point of redshirting is so that the student can learn the system and develop their skills without having to give up a year of eligibility on the field.

In the next season, Russell initially split his time with senior Daniel Evans and junior Harrison Beck. Eventually, he led the team to a four game winning streak in 2008. He was able to throw for 201 yards and three touchdowns in a game against East Carolina.

However, Russell suffered a momentary defeat when his team played against Rutgers and he was awkwardly hit. It was concluded that he suffered a knee sprain in the first half of the game. Due to his injury, Russell had to sit for the remainder of the game. His replacement threw three interceptions and the team eventually lost by the score of 23-29.

For the entirety of the 2008 season, Russell completed 17 total touchdown passes. He was named the first team All-ACC quarterback by the Atlantic Coast Conference. It was the very first time that a freshman was given that title. Needless go say, Russell was beginning to draw attention to himself and his team because of his amazing play out on the field. North Carolina State fans were ecstatic, because they hadn't expected Russell to develop so early in his college career.

During the next season, Russell continued to shine. He broke Andre Wilson's record of 325 consecutive passes without an interception. He held the title until Colby Cameron, of Louisiana Tech, broke it in November of 2012. Wilson completed college at NC State after three years with a degree in Communications. The season was a solid one for both Russell and the Wolfpack, as the team ended the campaign with a 9-4 record. However, Russell wasn't a top 10 prospect for scouts, and he wasn't receiving much hype upon season's end. Russell did not even receive an invite to the 2011 NFL Scouting Combine.

Because of the disappointment of not getting much scouting attention, combined with the chance to become a professional baseball player, Russell reported to spring training for the Colorado Rockies organization. After not feeling completely fulfilled in baseball, Russell decided he wanted to try to prove himself again on the football field.

Russell committed to the University of Wisconsin for the 2011 college football season. Because he redshirted his freshman season, he still had one season of eligibility left in his collegiate career. Russell completed 255 passes, and lead the team to victory with a great overall season. Wisconsin received heavy media attention and was showcased on multiple nationally-televised games. This helped to take Russell's skills and reputation to the next level.

By the end of the season, he was named to the All-Big Ten team in the coaches' poll. He also continued to win awards like the Griese-Brees Big Ten Quarterback of the Year award. A turning point in Russell's collegiate career came when he led the team to a victory against the Michigan State Spartans during the Big Ten Championship Game in December of 2011.

However, the biggest highlight of the year came when Wisconsin earned a bid to the historic Rose Bowl to play the Oregon Ducks. This was huge for the school, and gave the country a chance to see Russell set the single season FBS record for passing efficiency. Wisconsin lost the game by a touchdown, but it helped to put Wisconsin back in the discussion of college football powerhouse teams.

After such a prestigious collegiate career at two different universities, Russell had proven that he could possibly help a professional team as a quarterback at the next level. Once again, the most impressive attribute that Russell showed in his time at Wisconsin was his ability to lead. Entering a situation where he was a new face on a team that already had high expectations, Russell proved he could take charge of a locker room and get a team to buy into his decision-making on the field.

Chapter 3:

Professional Life

Russell Wilson's professional career started when he was still enrolled in college. By January of 2012, he began training for the NFL Scouting Combine at IMG Madden Football Academy.

Prior to his recruitment, Russell was already being evaluated by many scouts. The director of the IMG Football Academy commented that the only reason Wilson was not an immediate first round choice for teams was because of his height. However, in April of 2012, he was chosen by the Seattle Seahawks in the third round.

Five quarterbacks were selected ahead of Russell in the Draft. Andrew Luck from Stanford was actually the number one draft selection for the year, followed by Heisman trophy winner Robert Griffin III at second. The other quarterbacks chosen ahead of Wilson in that draft were Ryan Tannehill, Brandon Weeden, and finally Brock Osweiler. With the exception of Osweiler, all the quarterbacks started the 2012 season as their team's starting quarterback. This quarterback class was one of the strongest in decades.

Rookie Year

After qualifying for the team, Russell signed a contract with the Seahawks worth $2.99 million over the course of his first 4 seasons.

By the end of August, he was already named the starting quarterback for the team, after competing with Matt Flynn and Tavaris Jackson. He made his regular season debut in September, but unfortunately lost against the Arizona Cardinals. During the third regular season game, the team won against the Green Bay Packers with a controversial Hail Mary pass to Golden Tate. The referees' questionable decision was said to have led to an agreement to end the NFL referee lockout.

Russell was awarded the Pepsi NFL Rookie of the Week award for his performance. He was also praised for leading his team to victory over the New York Jets, a game in which he completed 12 out of 19 pass attempts for 188 yards, along with two touchdowns. He was later named the NFC Offensive Player of the Week, as well as the FedEx Player of the Week. He subsequently earned the award of Rookie of the Month from the NFL. Not a bad start to a career!

Russell finished his rookie season in fourth place on the NFL passer rating chart, becoming the highest rated rookie quarterback in NFL history. He continued to put up excellent performances that were compared to those of Fran Tarkenton, a legendary Hall of Fame Quarterback.

After qualifying for the NFC Playoffs as a Wild Card team, Russell led the Seahawks against the Washington Redskins, and eventually won by a 24-14 score. They advanced to the next round of the playoffs to battle the Atlanta Falcons, but unfortunately lost the game.

To cap off the great season, Russell was chosen as an alternate for the 2013 Pro Bowl, where he completed 8 out of 10 attempts and scored three touchdowns. He even earned a $222,000 bonus by the end of the season because of his impressive performances.

While the Seahawks would have liked to have gotten to the Super Bowl, it was obvious upon season's end that the future of the franchise looked bright. With Russell turning into a star, along with other young talent such as Richard Sherman, there was a lot of hype for what Seattle could become. Many people even predicted that Seattle could be the favorite, along with the San Francisco 49ers, to come out of the NFC in the following year.

Super Bowl Season

Russell came out to play in the 2013 season, showing that there was going to be no sophomore jinx. His almost flawless play at the start of the season led Seattle to its first ever 4-0 start. After a loss to Indianapolis, Seattle romped off another seven straight wins, capping it with Russell's three-touchdown performance in a 34-7 defeat of Drew Brees and the New Orleans Saints. Russell won the NFC Offensive Player of the Week award in Week 13, the only Seahawk to be recognized for that award.

The Seahawks would eventually secure the best record in the NFC, at 13-3, and the top seed in the playoffs. So how good was Russell Wilson? In a year in which veteran quarterbacks Peyton Manning, Drew Brees, and Philip Rivers were having close to career seasons, Russell became the first quarterback in the Super Bowl era to post a 100 or higher passer rating in his first two seasons in the league. He was also selected to the Pro Bowl for the second consecutive season, and finished ahead of Tom Brady, Eli Manning, and Aaron Rodgers in touchdown passes.

Russell and the Seahawks did not let up in the playoffs, although they were stiffly challenged by the San Francisco 49ers and the New Orleans Saints on the way to the Super Bowl game. Russell was efficient in playing the general role in the two playoff wins, not throwing an interception or fumbling the ball, while using his mobility and deft running skills to evade sacks and prolong plays.

He made sure that the Seahawks would not have to walk the tightrope in their first two playoff wins. In the final game of the season, Russell threw for two touchdowns, without throwing for an interception, passed for 206 yards, and rushed for 36, as the Seahawks crushed Peyton Manning and the Broncos, 43-8. He outplayed Manning, posting a 123.1 passer rating for the game, becoming just the second African-American quarterback to lead his team to a Super Bowl win.

Russell Wilson typified the Seattle Seahawks - young, brash, and confident, and people were talking "dynasty" often, revolving around a superstar quarterback. John Elway, Tom Brady, and Peyton Manning came to mind in leading teams to playoff excellence for a long period of time, and Russell Wilson, despite being 5'11" and not a top selection in the Draft, apparently had the tools and the character to be among these greats.

Back to the Super Bowl!

The Seahawks slipped very little from their previous season. They won 3 of their first 4 games, and while they didn't have a 7-game winning streak like they did in their first Super Bowl season, they closed out the regular season with 6 straight wins, sweeping the 5 games in their division, cruising by at least ten points in every win.

In a rematch of the previous year's Super Bowl, Russell once against faced Peyton Manning and the Denver Broncos on September 21st, 2014. And as in the prior year's championship game, Russell delivered once again. He marched the Seahawks on an 80-yard touchdown drive in overtime to defeat the Denver Broncos, 26–20. In the game, he passed for 288 yards and completed two touchdowns, while also running for 49 yards; and once again topping Manning in passer rating.

In a December game against the Arizona Cardinals, Russell would put together another memorable performance, throwing two touchdowns, and rushing for another, while passing for a career high 339 yards, completing 21 out 30 attempts. He also set a franchise record by gaining 596 total yards in a game. With Russell leading the offense, the Seahawks once again finished the regular season as the NFC's top seed.

Russell had another impressive individual campaign, but it was not a spectacular rise from the previous year. He failed to post a 100+ passer rating for the third consecutive year, and had the fewest regular season touchdowns (20) in his early career. On the positive side, he posted his third consecutive increase in passing yards, and threw the least amount of interceptions (7), in his three-year professional career.

The road to the Super Bowl was following a familiar script for Russell. In the Divisional Round, Seattle routed Cam Newton and the Carolina Panthers, 31-17, as they became the first defending Super Bowl champion since New England in 2005 to win a playoff game, indicating how hard it is to excel as a team right after winning the Big Game. To add to the celebration, Russell played a near perfect game, passing for 268 yards and 3 touchdowns, connecting on 67% of his passes, and did not throw an interception.

In the NFC title game, the Green Bay Packers, led by Aaron Rodgers, visited the Seahawks, and for the first time in his young playoff career, Russell struggled mightily, showing that he might be human after all – he threw 3 interceptions in the first half alone, completing only 2 passes, as the defending champions fell behind, 16-0. The hometown fans' hearts sank further when he threw his fourth interception of the game with just 5 minutes left, and Green Bay leading by two scores, 19-7. It looked like the cape had been removed from Russell Wilson's Superman persona.

But Russell would not disappoint, and saved his best for last. On the Seahawks' next series, he ran a touchdown in by himself from the goal line on a third down. After Green Bay sent the game into overtime, Russell passed for 80 yards in the extra session, including the winning touchdown pass, as Seattle marched back into the Super Bowl in quite dramatic fashion, 28-22. Russell had just led Seattle to their best playoff comeback in franchise history.

The Seahawks became the only team since the 2004 New England Patriots to return to the Super Bowl after a previous championship year. In Super Bowl XLIX, Russell had another efficient game, throwing for two touchdowns and passing for 234 yards, without throwing an interception, at least for the first 59 minutes, and 35 seconds of the game.   With New England up 28-24, Seattle had possession on the Patriot's 1 yard line with 26 seconds to go.

Instead of giving running back Marshawn Lynch 3 chances to run the one yard for the win, Seattle instead asked Russell to pass at the goal line. On the very next play, Russell would make the biggest mistake of his career, throwing an interception to Malcolm Butler, as the Seahawks' back-to-back Super Bowl chances came to a screeching halt.

Fourth Season

It seemed that the previous year's loss deflated Seattle and their broken hearts would continue through Russell's fourth year in the NFL. The Seahawks started their season poorly, losing their two opening games, and recovered at 4-4 by midseason. Their mediocre start, however, had nothing to do with the play of Russell.

He had an incredible statistical year and his arm and running led the Seahawks to the second round of the playoffs, eventually falling to the juggernaut that was the Carolina Panthers, which would eventually be the Super Bowl runner-up.

Russell achieved new career highs in passing touchdowns (a franchise all-time best of 34); passing completions, attempts, and passing percentage; passing yards (a franchise all-time best of 4,024), and passing yards per attempt; career highs in pass completions, completion percentage, passing attempts, passing yards/attempt, and passer rating, where he actually led the league with 110.1! Russell's passer rating was also a franchise high for the Seattle Seahawks.

He was also highly effective on the ground, where he posted his second highest season totals in rushing yards and rushing attempts, trailing only Thomas Rawls in team rushing yards. Among NFL quarterbacks, Russell had the third highest rushing total for the regular season.

In his career year, Russell set NFL records for being the first NFL quarterback in history to throw at least three passing touchdowns in five straight games, and also the first NFL quarterback in history to post a passer rating of at least 128 in five straight games.

To top off his incredible statistical year, Russell became the first NFL quarterback in history to pass for over 30 touchdowns and 4,000 yards, and run for at least 500 yards in the same year.

However, being the consummate professional, Russell was not one to rest on his achievements. Immediately after their season ended in the form of a playoff blowout to the Panthers, he sat down with his coach, Pete Carroll, and agreed to focus on the defensive side of the game in the offseason.

They agreed that looking at defensive schemes and rotations would widen Russell's focus. With regard to focus, and the mental aspect of football, Russell himself said that there is also room for improvement in that area. He says that the key to even being a better player is to grow intellectually, and being able to master that aspect of the game. He says that the game slows down significantly when a player possesses a tight mental grasp on the game.

Football Secrets

Aside from the strong mental discipline, according to analysts and coaches, there are a few obvious unique contributing factors to Russell's success on the football field. They are:

Play-Action Pass

There is a big difference between a running quarterback, and quarterback who can run, and Russell is squarely in the second category of quarterbacks who run when they have to.

A famous quarterback, Warren Moon, praised Russell's ability to perfect the play-action pass, which is a fake handoff that allows him to get the defense to bite or even better, freeze altogether. Because of his height, Russell needs to distance himself from the offensive linemen in order to see other receivers downfield. His agility has allowed him to master fakes and keep his opponents at bay.

Agility, however, is only a component of Russell's success as a play action quarterback. He spends a lot of time studying his opponents' defensive schemes, as well as identifying players' weaknesses on the opponents' defensive line. He has often been named as one of the top three play-action quarterbacks in the NFL, together with Cam Newton and Ryan Tannehill. Russell has dazzled NFL observers by his dual weapons of being able to scramble effectively off the snap, and having the arm to throw long bombs downfield while on the move.

The Seahawks' reliance on play-action has unwittingly led to an increase in Russell's rushing statistics over his first three years in the league. In 2015, Russell had less rush attempts and a lower yards per rush average, which many attribute to the Seahawks' less than stellar offensive line work in the first half of the season. As a result, Russell was sacked a career high 45 times, and relied more on passing plays.

Teamwork

Much of Russell's game is reliant on his teammates. In the second quarter of the NFC Wild Card game against the Washington Redskins, the Seahawks managed to slip past blockers by using Marshawn Lynch as a blocker for Wilson. Thanks to Coach Carroll's brilliance, Russell's teammates also help to hide some of his weaknesses.

On the other hand, Russell's ability to scramble after a botched play-action helps mask deficiencies in the offensive line, and his receivers not being in position for designed plays.

Strong Physique

Speaking of weaknesses, strength isn't one for Russell. Despite being the shortest starting quarterback in the NFL, Russell has one of the strongest arms. He can throw the ball behind opposing safeties without any problem. He has successfully helped to break stigmas attached to the myth of short quarterbacks not being able to succeed, following in the footsteps of others before him, like Drew Brees.

Russell also has large hands, which allow him to hold the ball tighter and throw it with greater velocity. In his rookie combine, they measured his hands to be the fourth largest among quarterbacks; he has hands even bigger than those of some defensive linemen almost a foot taller than he is. Because of his size, Russell is also not prone to being tackled as much. New regulations on body contact also increase his advantage, since players are no longer allowed to hit quarterbacks below the knees.

He is also praised for being a great strategist with a lot of patience. Some quarterbacks panic whenever they are feeling pressure in the pocket, but Russell has an uncanny ability to slip in and out of the pocket, while still keeping his eyes downfield.

Probably the most important of all is the fact that Russell continuously makes smart, safe decisions, which allow him to avoid unnecessary hits. Many athletic quarterbacks rely on their athleticism too much and end up getting injured by trying to make "hero" plays. Despite being athletic enough to make plays himself, Russell prefers to use his athleticism to buy time and give the ball to the other play-makers on his team.

Aside from his strong physique, Russell is one of the fastest, if not the fastest, quarterback in the NFL despite his height. In the pre-draft NFL combine, Russell ran the 40-yard dash in just over 4.5 seconds.

Baseball Career

Russell played both football and baseball professionally. He was selected as a member of the Baltimore Orioles after graduating from high school, but chose to attend NC State instead. Russell was a member of the NC State Wolfpack baseball team from 2008 until 2010. In a game against the Gastonia Grizzlies, he posted a total of five home runs.

Russell was drafted by the Colorado Rockies in the fourth round, and played as a second baseman for the Tri-City Dust Devils, where he posted a batting average of .230. In 2011, he played 61 games for the Asheville Tourists, an affiliate of the Colorado Rockies. He totaled three home runs and a batting average of .228. In the beginning of 2012, he finally informed the Rockies that he would be devoting his time to pursuing a career in the NFL, and would not be able to play the 2012 season.

Even when he was already playing in the NFL, Major League Baseball teams continued to move in on him. On December 12th, 2013, the Texas

Rangers acquired Russell from the Rockies. He continued to attend the Rangers' spring training camps in Arizona in 2014 and 2015.

Money Man

Russell's brilliance has led to financial success for the little guy that nobody wanted in 2012. As the 75th selection in the Draft, Russell eventually became the NFL's lowest paid starting quarterback with a base salary of $390,000 per year.

But four years of on-the-field brilliance, combined with his winning personality, would pay off. After the 2015 season, Russell re-signed with the Seahawks for four years, where he will earn a total of $87,600,000, including a whopping $31,000,000 signing bonus. Of this amount, $61,542,000 is guaranteed, and he will earn an average annual salary of $21,900,000. In 2016, Russell will earn a base salary of $12,342,000, to go up to $17,000,000 in 2019, just as he will be turning thirty years old. But Russell's football compensation is just the start of the financial windfall.

Russell selected his "advertising" company wisely. Right after being drafted in 2012, he announced that he had selected

French/West/Vaughan as his marketing company, responsible for his public relations and product endorsement deals. The relatively new company, founded in 1997, had NFL players in their client base, and Russell felt this was a good sign that they knew the industry.

As for his endorsement potential, Russell is a Super Bowl winner with a squeaky-clean image, and sports marketing experts predict he is putting himself in position to be the new face of the NFL. It helps that the hottest quarterbacks of the last several years are riding into the sunset, relinquishing their own endorsement deals at the same time, so advertisers are looking for fresh blood to hawk their clients' products.

Peyton Manning, Drew Brees, and Tom Brady are practically done with their careers; while others like Aaron Rodgers are on the far side of thirty years old. Russell and the changing quarterback guard of the NFL are more than willing to fill the void.

French/West/Vaughan would not disappoint. Immediately after winning the Seahawks's starting quarterback job in September 2012,

Russell filmed his first commercial for jeans maker, Levi's.

A few months later, he signed a two-year endorsement contract with American Family Insurance, appearing in television commercials for the company. French/West/Vaughan also signed him for advertising deals with Seattle-based Microsoft and Alaska Airlines, Duracell batteries, Bose, United Way, Braun, and Pepsi. Forbes Magazine recently estimated his endorsement earnings to be in the neighborhood of $6.5 million -- amazingly ahead of Tom Brady.

In 2014, Russell became part-owner and endorser of Eat the Ball, an Austrian bread company marketing pre-baked frozen bread. Eat the Ball has been making a substantial push into the American market, with Russell as one of their prime endorsers.

In 2015, he began endorsing Luvo, another frozen food company, and Reliant Recovery Water, a $3-per-bottle mixture containing electrolytes and "nanobubbles", which supposedly help people to recover quickly from workouts.

Of course, Russell is also the biggest active sports figure in Seattle, a city with just two major professional teams, and he is clearly the face of the Seahawks. His face is literally on signage all over the city, including a local car endorsement with a Mercedes dealership.

Chapter 4:

Personal Adult Life

Despite becoming a successful athlete, Russell remains grounded and has maintained a strong relationship with his family.

Faith

Russell is a devout Christian and has considered faith an important part of his life. He posts Bible verses most days via his personal Twitter account. He acknowledged that faith became the foundation for his family when he was growing up.

In a blog entitled "The Makings of a Champion", Russell described how he became a Christian. The quarterback said that an important part of his Christian belief came when he was just 14 years old. He was a very "angry" boy before coming to a football camp, and he dreamt that his father had died, and that he needed to get right with Jesus. In the dream, Jesus knocked on his door and told him that he needed to learn more about his faith. He immediately replaced his tantrums and anger with focus.

While the Wilsons regularly attended Sunday mass, it was that particular dream that moved Russell to become a follower of Christ. Russell also said that he felt the dream turned out to be a prophecy, because his father died six years later.

Russell also talks about the influence of God in relation to on-the-field issues. In the 2014 Conference Championship Game, Russell had thrown four interceptions and had his team down by two scores with under four minutes left. He led the team on a comeback and said that it was God that set the situation up, and that God had made it so that the game's ending would be much more special, dramatic, and rewarding. Russell has absolute and incontrovertible faith in a higher power. He believes that God will make him overcome any obstacle - and this gives him power to proceed despite obstacles.

Chapter 5:

Philanthropic and Charitable Acts

both

Russell is an active member of the Seattle community. He regularly visits the Children's Hospital in Seattle, and also visits soldiers at the Lewis-McChord camp.

both

The Seahawks' fans now have a greater reason to cheer for Russell Wilson, because he received an incentive to complete as many touchdowns as possible. For every touchdown, Russell will donate $2,000 to the Wilson's charitable foundation, which supports youth activities. Russell accumulated a total of 30 touchdowns last season and if he repeats this performance, he will be able to raise $60,000 by the end of the next season.

CR3 Diabetes Association

Russell also agreed to be a National Ambassador for the CR3 Diabetes Association. Russell's father, Harrison, suffered a series of complications due to diabetes. Ultimately, this contributed to his death in 2010. As he watched his own father suffer, Russell felt the pressing need to help others once he reached the NFL.

CR3 Diabetes Association provides medical supplies to those who cannot afford them. They also provide tools that can monitor the blood sugar levels of diabetics. The program greatly encourages people to take control of their lives and help others who are great candidates for treatment.

The Duct Tape Wallet

One of the most popular stories about Russell's charitable work centers around a duct tape wallet made by an 11 year old Seahawks fan. Allison Christensen was admitted to the Children's Hospital that Russell regularly visits after being diagnosed with a heart condition.

The girl's interest in sports was very evident by her Seahawks-decorated room. The hospital put her on the list of patients to meet the quarterback, who goes to the hospital every Tuesday. She was very excited, and spent time to create a special duct tape wallet for Russell.

Allison has been making the wallets to pass the time and to help her family with the hospital bills. As soon as the quarterback entered her room, Allison could not erase the smile off of her face. When she gave him the wallet, he was so enthralled that he couldn't erase his smile either.

However, they didn't really expect it to create such a huge sensation over the next few days.

Russell proudly showed his new wallet in a press conference, which attracted media attention. At the same time, Allison finally received news that she would be getting a heart transplant, which went well.

Russell Wilson Passing Academy

Russell runs a youth football camp for kids 9-17 years old that, not only provides instruction on football fundamentals, but also encourages the physical and mental development of its participants, and a sense of fair play within the atmosphere of competitiveness.

The camp aims to develop in children a sense of impeccable character, an awareness of moral standards with the goal of encouraging kids to develop high character and moral standards, service to others, and respect for authority.

In keeping with his own personal experience, Russell also wants the camp to instill a love of God, country, and family in its participants. Sponsors also pitch in so that underprivileged and inner-city youth can participate.

Chapter 6:

Legacy and Inspiration

Russell is just starting to create his own legacy in football. However, he has already attracted the attention of many football fans around the globe.

Size Doesn't Matter

One of the reasons that Russell has become relatable is because of his height. During the 2012 NFL Draft, most scouts and so-called experts paraded a list of quarterbacks less than six feet tall who never made it in the NFL. Many teams did not notice him immediately, because he wasn't as tall as other quarterbacks.

However, instead of giving up on his dream, Russell used this as motivation to become a better player and develop other skills to compensate.

Know Your Goals and Stick to Them

Watching his father and grandfather succeed in life, Russell realized early on that a true leader must have goals, not only for him, but for his team. Russell does not hesitate when asked what his goals are: Be consistent, be dominant, perform well in clutch situations, and try to stay healthy.

He urges everyone who will listen that a person should affix these goals into their consciousness so that they become part of a person's every action.

Power of Education

Although Russell is a true athlete at heart, he is also fundamentally powered by education. His father was an athlete himself, but he was also an accomplished lawyer, who dedicated time to teach his son not only about sports, but also about life and the world.

Even during the NFL season, Russell puts in a lot of time studying playbooks and video to improve his game, understand the competition, and make his team better.

Most people from his family had to work their way through college and the same principle was instilled in Russell. No matter how busy he was with football and baseball practice, he always made sure he had time for school work. As a result, he graduated from college with his bachelors degree in only three years.

A Driven Player

Russell's success has paved the way for many opportunities for himself and for the people he helps. The company that handles his advertising campaigns, French/West/Vaughan, says that the football superstar has many endorsement deal offerings, but he insists on limiting them in order to concentrate more on his sport.

Russell's achievements are not just a product of luck and good genes. He also worked very hard to be the player he is today. Just like any serious athlete, he also undergoes serious training to prepare his body for the physical challenges that come with playing football for up to twenty games a year.

Take Your Chances

Russell took a great risk when he left baseball, because he was also good enough to play in the big leagues, and didn't know what the future would hold. But he also understood that playing baseball professionally wasn't the same as playing football professionally, not to him.

His ultimate goal as an athlete was to become the best football player he could, and he had to make certain sacrifices in order to accomplish that goal. He took a risk and the possibility of him missing out on an NFL career was a real possibility. Regardless, he stayed true to himself and did not change course just because he may have been perceived negatively by others.

Have A Big Heart

Russell has been known to go out of his way to help people in need. Most of the people that meet him also notice that he treats everyone with such kindness, which is rare to see in a professional athlete.

Russell is a man of faith and has tremendous confidence in his skill and has continued to prove his excellence. He also doesn't have any problem sharing his spiritual views to others. He relies strongly on his faith and is not afraid to tell anyone about it. Perhaps this is also one of the contributing factors to his grounded disposition.

Don't Make Excuses

After their Super Bowl loss, Russell didn't make excuses for his bad pass, but instead defended the Seahawks coaching staff, which was getting a lot of heat for calling the "wrong" play. Russell said after the game that, "When they made the call, I didn't question it", and that he thought they were going to win the game.

This ability to take the blame for the team is something we can all learn from. Rather than looking to point the finger at others when we come up short, we can be more like Russell and always take responsibility for what we could have done better - in any situation. This is a very admirable trait and by becoming this kind of individual, people around us will feel a great deal of respect for us.

Pay Attention To The Little Details

Success in the NFL is sometimes measured in inches, or fractions of a second. Russell recognizes this, and does not take anything for granted.

Whether he is managing the clock, feeling the creases on the ball, or noticing a defensive lineman's minute shift of position, Russell makes sure that he focuses on the little things, realizing that nothing can be taken for granted in the cutthroat profession that he is in.

Don't Give Up and Maintain A Positive Attitude

Losses and disappointments come and go, and those who fail are those who stumble, and stay down. One of the life lessons from Russell's story is that when one is faced with adversity, that person just can't give up. Life is full of failure, adversity, and tough tests of character.

In order to succeed in life, one has to learn from his/her mistakes. Russell believes that defeats and setbacks are simply just a preparation for better things to come. It is these defeats and setbacks in life that set people up for success. Life is about rising again after being knocked down, and a positive mental attitude is key to helping one bounce back after being knocked to the ground.

After the Super Bowl loss, Russell went on the next season to have another career year. He has said on more than one occasion that he has had so many some ups and downs, but that still he goes on win or lose, succeed or fail.

Life Isn't All About Us... Glorify Others!

Russell is humble enough to realize that rather than being a gift to mankind, he instead realizes he has been given gifts to help mankind. He understands that humans were placed on Earth so that they share their rewards and gifts with others, especially with those who have less. He also understands that these gifts should be shared through compassion, love, and encouragement.

For Russell, this seems to be accomplished by offering his time, money, and effort to local and even, national hospitals and charities. But more than giving away money and time, Russell also gives away the glory.

He realizes that no matter how good he is individually, he is only as good as his teammates allow him to be, and he always redirects the attention, praise, and glory thrown his way. He is the consummate team man, and has dealt with what many football experts say, as a mediocre offensive line in some instances, not by blaming them for failures, but uplifting his play to make his teammates better.

As a quarterback, he becomes the natural center of attention of a football team. In interviews, he more often than not heaves praise onto his receivers, his offensive line, defensive line, and even the coaching staff. To him, winning is a team effort, and not surprisingly for a man like him, he takes personal responsibility for his team's losses.

Prepare, Prepare, Prepare

Russell is a study in concentration off the field as well. There are very few players who take as much time before a game to prepare for his opponents, allowing him to be as ready as he can be on game day.

His focus leads him to spend endless hours studying film, and reviewing the Seahawks' playbook to enable him to figure out how he can move better on the field, and stump the opposing team. To the average fan, many think that his excellence and often flawless play is because of pure natural ability.

The truth is, by taking painstaking time to prepare for games, Russell is always knowledgeable on the other team's tendencies and the strengths and weaknesses of his own team's personnel for the week.

Conclusion

Hopefully this book was able to help you gain inspiration from the life of Russell Wilson, one of the best quarterbacks currently playing in the National Football League.

The rise and fall of a star is often cause for much wonder, but most stars have an expiration date. In football, once a star player reaches his mid- to late-thirties, it is often time to contemplate retirement. What will be left in people's minds about that fading star? In Russell Wilson's case, people will remember how he led his team in their journey to a Super Bowl. He will be remembered as the guy who defied all odds, helping the team build their image again, and honing his own image along the way.

Russell has also inspired so many people because he is the star who never failed to look back, who paid his dues forward by helping thousands of less-fortunate youth find their inner light through sports and education.

Another thing that stands out in Russell's story is the fact that he never forgot where he came from. As soon as he had the capacity to give back, he poured what he had straight back to those who needed it, and he continues to do so to this day.

Russell Wilson is one of the most captivating talents in football today. Noted for his ability to impose his will on any game, he is a joy to watch on the football field. At the same time, he is one of the nicest guys outside the gridiron, willing to help out teammates and give back to fans. Last but not least, he's remarkable for remaining simple and firm with his principles in spite of his immense popularity.

Hopefully you've learned some great things about Russell in this book, and are able to apply some of the lessons you've learned to your own life! Good luck in your journey!

CPSIA information can be obtained
at www.ICGtesting.com
Printed in the USA
BVHW041144310120
571104BV00012B/68

9 781508 427360